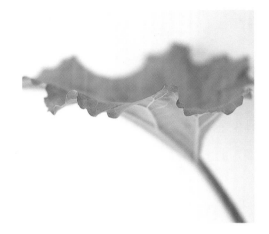

spring
cooking

BRIDGET JONES

using the season's finest ingredients

spring cooking

LORENZ BOOKS

This edition is published by Lorenz Books

Lorenz Books is an imprint of Anness Publishing Ltd
Hermes House, 88–89 Blackfriars Road, London SE1 8HA
tel. 020 7401 2077; fax 020 7633 9499
www.lorenzbooks.com; info@anness.com

© Anness Publishing Ltd 2003

This edition distributed in the UK by Aurum Press Ltd,
25 Bedford Avenue, London WC1B 3AT; tel. 020 7637 3225; fax 020 7580 2469

This edition distributed in the USA and Canada by National Book Network, 4720 Boston
Way, Lanham, MD 20706; tel. 301 459 3366; fax 301 459 1705; www.nbnbooks.com

This edition distributed in Australia by Pan Macmillan Australia, Level 18, St Martins
Tower, 31 Market St, Sydney, NSW 2000; tel. 1300 135 113; fax 1300 135 103;
customer.service@macmillan.com.au

This edition distributed in New Zealand by David Bateman Ltd, 30 Tarndale Grove,
Off Bush Road, Albany, Auckland; tel. (09) 415 7664; fax (09) 415 8892

A CIP catalogue record for this book is available from the British Library.

PUBLISHER: Joanna Lorenz
MANAGING EDITOR: Judith Simons
PROJECT EDITOR: Katy Bevan
DESIGNER: Adelle Morris
EDITORIAL READER: Jay Thundercliffe
PRODUCTION CONTROLLER: Joanna King
COVER PHOTOGRAPHY: Martin Brigdale
PHOTOGRAPHERS: Caroline Arber, Tim Auty, Martin Brigdale, Michelle Garrett,
Amanda Heywood, William Lingwood, Thomas Odulate, Craig Robertson
RECIPES: Alex Barker, Angela Boggiano, Jacqueline Clark, Matthew Drennan,
Joanna Farrow, Brian Glover, Nicola Graimes, Becky Johnson, Lucy Knox,
Sara Lewis, Maggie Mayhew, Keith Richmond, Rena Salaman, Anne Sheasby,
Marlena Spieler, Linda Tubby, Kate Whiteman, Jeni Wright

10 9 8 7 6 5 4 3 2 1

NOTES
Bracketed terms are intended for
American readers.

For all recipes, quantities are given in both
metric and imperial measures and, where
appropriate, measures are also given in
standard cups and spoons. Follow one set,
but not a mixture, because they are not
interchangeable.

Standard spoon and cup measures are level.
1 tsp = 5ml, 1 tbsp = 15ml, 1 cup = 250ml/8fl oz

Australian standard tablespoons are 20ml.
Australian readers should use 3 tsp in place
of 1 tbsp for measuring small quantities of
gelatine, flour, salt, etc.

Medium (US large) eggs are used unless
otherwise stated.

CONTENTS

INTRODUCTION

Spring is a wonderfully positive season. Lengthening days and brighter weather bring a sense of energy that influences appetite as well as activity. Young produce is just becoming available from local suppliers and many garden owners have rows of tiny vegetables ready for thinning out and sampling. Pots of herbs on a sheltered patio produce an abundance of new shoots to bring fresh and lively flavours to simple cooking. There are several good reasons for bothering to find seasonal specialities: from a purely culinary angle, the fresher the food, the better its condition and flavour, and the easier it is to cook; fresh food is more nutritious, because the vitamin value diminishes with staleness; and last, but by no means least, buying food in season can be economical.

Special in spring

Sunlight, warmth and spring rain encourage rapid growth, and it is difficult to resist the temptation to pick too many seedlings or young shoots from a vegetable plot or herb tub. While the average garden offers a small yield, commercial growers have brought on their produce to fill the shelves and markets with crisp young vegetables.

BABY VEGETABLES

Look for little leeks, spring onions (scallions) and spring greens (collards): these deliciously tender young leaves grow from cut cabbage stumps to provide oodles of versatile flavour for little cost. Tall purple sprouting broccoli is absolutely bursting with flavour, but its season is short, so catch it while you can. The first leaves of Swiss chard, young spinach and sorrel go well together or separately in salads or cooked dishes.

Baby carrots are irresistibly sweet and their tender tops are deliciously fresh in salads or used herb-style in cooked dishes. Young broad (fava) beans come into the

shops and the small pods are a particular treat. Globe artichokes also feature; look for young Italian vegetables in which the chokes have not yet formed, and cook them whole. Young peas and tender mangetouts (snow peas) are full of flavour.

Young vine leaves are readily available outdoors in some regions or from a greenhouse vine in cooler areas. A short spell of hot weather brings up the asparagus shoots and it is time to indulge at the first signs because the season is short.

Fresh mint and chives sprout up to become the favourite spring herbs but there is also new growth on established plants, such as bay, rosemary and sage.

TENDER MEAT AND FISH

Spring lamb is the seasonal star – tender, sweet cutlets (rib chops) are perfect for grilling (broiling) while racks and legs make succulent and aromatic roasts. Traditionally, spring is also the time for chicken, especially young spring chicken or poussin. Guinea fowl is a good choice for a lighter style of casserole: it is at its prime at this time of year.

The availability of local fish and seafood depends on the weather, but there is always a good choice of white or firm fish from around the world. Select flat fish, such as sole, plaice or flounder and make the most of shellfish for delicate flavour and texture, opting for firm tuna for main dishes that are satisfying without being over-rich.

REFRESHING SWEETS

Rhubarb is the vegetable that is treated as a fruit in culinary terms. Forced rhubarb is available in early spring, followed by the main crop which will be past its edible best by summer. The tart, fruity stalks make tempting puddings and refreshing desserts. There are still juicy seedless oranges and zesty thin-skinned lemons to add a citrus lift to savoury and sweet cooking giving recipes a light spring feel.

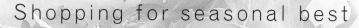

Shopping for seasonal best

Making the most of seasonal produce is all about selective shopping – checking out the source of supply and picking through produce to find succulent new roots, shoots and leaves that are bursting with spring goodness.

Reading labels may not be the most romantic of selection methods but it is a first step to making the right choice. As well as the country of origin, the location of the grower is often included – you may well have the choice of purchasing produce that was harvested just a few miles away.

FARM SHOPS

Fields of green vegetables or crops of ripening fruit are sure signs that good local produce will soon be available, if it is not already on display. Major supermarket chains are extremely picky about the look of fruit and vegetables, accepting only model items of even size and form. This means that the slightly small, misshapen or irregular produce is often available in farm shops. While the "look" may be less than designer, the quality and flavour are usually excellent, and buying from the grower often ensures the items are fresh. It is also still possible to purchase at the farm gate in some areas – look out for signs indicating that seasonal crops are for sale.

SPECIALIST SUPPLIERS

Practical alternatives to supermarkets include specialist suppliers, such as fishmongers, butchers and delicatessens. Mail order and e-commerce along with fruit and vegetable box-schemes are popular means of trading. The quality is usually excellent and established companies ensure customers receive reliable deliveries.

MARKETS

Weekly markets are a feature of country towns and are great places to find quality at a good price. Whereas supermarkets prefer produce that is under-ripe and immature to allow for handling and long display, market traders usually offer fruit and vegetables that are ready for eating. The price is competitive and the quality is good, even if it does not have as long a shelf life. Local butchers, egg producers, fishmongers and cheese makers often have stalls at town markets.

Farmers' markets are not usually held as frequently as regular town markets – usually once or twice a month – but they bring together producers rather than the usual market retail traders. Shopping here provides the chance to quiz farmers (or their representatives, who may be selling on their behalf) about the way in which animals are reared, crops grown or food products manufactured. In turn, feedback and requests are usually welcome and this is a great way of establishing the sort of relationship our grandparents had with their shops and suppliers.

RICH PICKINGS

Garden produce, wild foods and pick-your-own outlets are the ultimate choices for freshness and economy. A vegetable patch is a source of relaxation as well as fabulous food and with the right planning it does not have to be overdemanding. Focusing on crops that thrive with the minimum of attention is perfectly possible – a local nursery or garden centre is the best source of advice. Even a small garden or patio can provide worthwhile reward for minimum attention. Vegetables, such as sprouting broccoli, beans and peas, can be grown in flower borders. Herbs bring a brilliant seasonal twist to dishes that may well be served throughout the year; grow them in flower beds or window boxes, hanging baskets or tubs, if a herb garden is not an option.

Culinary combinations

By tradition, spring is the season for fresh and lively combinations – bitter balanced by sweet, rich resolved by sharp. Success is found in speed and simplicity, a move away from the complex, long-cooked dishes of winter, taking care not to drown the first precious fresh produce and using the new herbs to enliven year-round foods. Try some of these flavours together with lighter styles of cooking like stir-frying and steaming.

- Use the first small vine leaves to cover the breast meat of poussin before roasting and serving with a salad of hot new potatoes with grapes and roast garlic cloves.

- Mint is the perfect foil for rich duck – use it in combination with lemon, lime or orange to enliven the pan juices from roasting or grilling (broiling) breast fillets. Add a little honey and cider vinegar for a sweet–sour balance.

- Give grilled or pan-fried pork a spring lift by sprinkling with chopped fresh mint and grated lime rind just before serving. Deglaze the pan juices with a little lime juice and a good pinch of sugar.

- Combine finely shredded spring greens (collards) and chard with chopped spring onions (scallions) and mint in a lively stir-fry vegetable base for serving pan-fried pork fillet.

- Make the most of baby new potatoes by serving them as the focus for a main-course salad. Toss the freshly cooked potatoes in a little olive oil, grated lemon rind and chopped chives, and then serve on a bed of baby spinach and garnish with chopped hard-boiled egg.

- Complement tender steamed broad (fava) beans with diced lean cooked ham and lots of chopped parsley for a first course or light lunch.

- Serve freshly cooked asparagus tips with creamy scrambled eggs and thin slices of crisp wholemeal (whole-wheat) toast for a superlative spring brunch.

- Blanch new potatoes until barely tender, and then skewer them with strips of prosciutto and brush with olive oil before grilling until golden.

- When purple sprouting broccoli is fresh and tender, serve the lightly boiled spears on a plain risotto flavoured with a little lemon and chives, and dress with melted butter.

- Rhubarb is delicious with lamb or duck: make a simple sauce of sliced rhubarb cooked with sugar until tender, then enrich it with a little port. Serve warm or cool as a condiment with roast lamb or duck.

- Select firm fish fillets or steaks for grilling, season lightly and serve topped with pats of simple lemon and chive butter. Add new potatoes and little mangetout (snow peas) or lightly steamed spinach.

- Warm salads are just right for spring and make a meal in themselves. Quickly pan-fry scallops in a little olive oil, toss gently and season well, and then pile on a large salad of shredded young spinach, tender young parsley sprigs, small whole mint leaves and chopped spring onions. Complement the flavours by adding some segments of orange, drizzle with a good salad dressing and serve at once.

A fresh approach

While hearty meals are still welcome on cool days, there is a universal urge to eat lighter dishes. Spring is a good time to ease gradually into a natural change of eating patterns.

VIBRANT SOUPS

Hot soup is still welcome, especially when it is enlivened with tender young vegetables in a light broth. Aim for a result that is finely cut and refreshing rather than overfilling. Garnish with finely shredded pancakes and chopped fresh herbs. When the weather is warmer, introduce cool soups that make the most of spring leaves and herbs in cooking.

STEAMING SPECIALITIES

Steaming is especially useful for lightening flavours and creating clean textures. Steam fish, vegetables or poultry wrapped in foil for maximum flavour retention. Include bay leaves, chives, parsley and the young fronds of fennel to taste. Strips of lemon, lime or orange rind, chopped spring onions (scallions) and fresh root ginger are lively additions.

LIGHT CASSEROLES

Select tender cuts – seafood, poultry or meat suitable for pan-frying – instead of tougher pieces that require hours in the oven. Sauté spring onions with a little celery and carrot before pan-frying the main ingredients. Use cider, white wine and chicken stock for light sauces and add baby vegetables towards the end of cooking so that they are still slightly crisp in the cooked casserole. Finally, instead of thickening the juices, use a slotted spoon to transfer the ingredients to a serving dish and reduce the cooking liquor to intensify its flavour by boiling rapidly in the open pan. Enrich it with a little cream, if you like, before pouring over the casserole ingredients.

SPEEDY STIR-FRIES

Lamb fillet, chicken breast and duck breast are ideal for stir-frying with aromatics and/or finely cut, tender vegetables. Balancing modest portions of meat with generous amounts of vegetables lightens meals. Instead of finishing stir-fries with thickened sauces, lace them with aromatic oil flavoured with garlic or chilli and wedges of lemon. Alternatively, try serving lightly stir-fried meat or fish on a bed of lettuce as a warm salad.

SUCCULENT GRILLS AND ROASTS

Marinate chops, fillets and steaks with olive oil, garlic, and orange rind and juice or a little balsamic vinegar before grilling (broiling). Complement with simple condiments of chopped herbs in plain yogurt – try finely shredded sorrel or chopped chives and mint.

Roast young lamb on a bed of rosemary and whole garlic cloves for fabulous flavour. Bring spring zest to roast chicken by lining the base of the roasting tin with sliced lemons and bay leaves and serve with fresh new potatoes.

Light on cooking

Young, new produce requires the minimum of attention, which means less kitchen time for more goodness on the plate. The following are essential techniques and basic cooking suggestions for a few spring specialities.

ASPARAGUS

Succulent young asparagus needs no more than washing. If the spears are long, snap or cut off any tough or woody ends, feeling along to where they break off easily. Cook young spears in a frying pan of simmering water for 5–7 minutes.

- Blanch young spears for 3 minutes, drain and brown in a little olive oil on a very hot griddle. Serve with lemon.

- Tie larger spears that need longer cooking in bundles and simmer in boiling water in a tall asparagus kettle or saucepan, keeping the tips out of the water (tent foil over the top of a pan if the asparagus stands above the rim). Allow 10–20 minutes.

SORREL

Tender, long sorrel leaves are similar in appearance to spinach. Their flavour is tangy and lemony. Sorrel is used to flavour sauces and stuffings, but the small young leaves are also good finely shredded in salads and make a delicious soup.

- Mix shredded sorrel into a salad of baby spinach and spring onions (scallions).

- Toss shredded sorrel into stir-fried finely sliced leeks.

BROAD/FAVA BEANS

Very young broad bean pods can be cooked whole. As the pods mature, the versatile beans inside can be cooked in many ways.

- Trim the ends off baby pods of broad beans and cook them whole in boiling water for 5 minutes, then serve with butter or olive oil.

- Cook shelled beans in boiling water for about 5 minutes. Blanch beans in boiling water for 2–3 minutes, or until just tender, then drain, rinse in cold water and remove the pale skins. Toss the bright green beans in a little butter or olive oil.

- Crumbled, crisp-grilled (broiled) prosciutto or crisp-fried pancetta is delicious with broad beans. Thyme, tarragon and summer savory are complementary herbs.

GLOBE ARTICHOKES

Whole baby young globe artichoke buds are edible before the choke forms. Trim off the stalk, any tough outer leaves and the tough tip, and then cut into quarters. Cook in boiling water for 5–10 minutes, or until tender. Alternatively, fry in butter or olive oil.

- To prepare a mature artichoke, slice off the top and discard the large, open outer leaves around the base. Snip off the points, then use a small sharp knife to remove the choke and surrounding yellow leaves from the middle. Drop into water, acidulated with a few drops of lemon or vinegar. Boil for 15–20 minutes, or until tender.

- When serving cold, remove the artichoke's outer leaves once cooked. Trim off the top and points, then ease back the leaves and pull out the yellow leaves and choke, easing it off the tender cooked base (heart) with a teaspoon.

SPRING ONIONS/SCALLIONS

Trim off the roots and tips of spring onions, then pan-fry them whole for about 1 minute in olive oil with lots of sliced garlic. Serve topped with lemon rind and chopped parsley or use as a topping for a dish of hot, boiled potatoes.

RHUBARB

Young slim rhubarb stalks are tender, and if sliced into short lengths they cook quickly in a little water with sugar – about 5 minutes' poaching is enough. Older stalks may be stringy and any tough strings should be peeled off. Allow 10 minutes to cook the larger pieces, being careful not to overcook into a pulp.

- Fresh root or dried powdered ginger complements rhubarb – add when cooking. Try adding orange rind in the pan when cooking.

- Use rhubarb in sweet pies, crumbles and baked puddings; cold rhubarb purée makes excellent creams, such as fruit fool.

- Rhubarb is excellent for chutneys and savoury sauces, especially in sweet–sour combinations.

young and crisp

As the days get longer and warmer, farmers' markets and local shops begin to stock a wider selection of mouthwatering spring produce. Enjoy first courses and side dishes that make the most of the new season's crisp shoots and tender herbs.

This delightful recipe transforms the classic wintry soup into a fresh-tasting and flavourful spring dish that is a celebration of these early vegetables.

SPRING MINESTRONE

INGREDIENTS
serves six

30ml | 2 tbsp olive oil

2 onions, finely chopped

2 garlic cloves, finely chopped

2 carrots, very finely chopped

1 celery stick, very finely chopped

1.3 litres | 2^1/$_4$ pints | 5^2/$_3$ cups boiling water

450g | 1lb | 2^1/$_2$ cups shelled fresh broad (fava) beans

225g | 8oz mangetouts (snow peas), cut into fine strips

3 tomatoes, peeled and chopped

5ml | 1 tsp tomato purée (paste)

50g | 2oz spaghettini, broken into 4cm | 1^1/$_2$in lengths

225g | 8oz baby spinach

30ml | 2 tbsp chopped fresh parsley

handful of fresh basil leaves

salt and ground black pepper

freshly grated Parmesan cheese, and sprigs of basil to serve

1 Heat the oil in a pan and add the onions and garlic. Cook for 4–5 minutes, or until softened. Add the carrots and celery, and cook for 2–3 minutes. Add the boiling water and simmer for 15 minutes, or until the vegetables are tender.

2 Cook the broad beans in salted boiling water for 4–5 minutes. Remove with a slotted spoon, refresh under cold water and set aside.

3 Bring the pan of water back to the boil, add the mangetouts and cook for 1 minute. Drain, then refresh under cold water and set aside.

4 Add the tomatoes and the tomato purée to the soup. Cook for 1 minute. Purée two or three large ladlefuls of the soup and a quarter of the broad beans in a food processor or blender until smooth. Set aside.

5 Add the spaghettini to the remaining soup and cook for 6–8 minutes until tender. Stir in the purée and spinach and cook for 2–3 minutes. Add the rest of the broad beans, the mangetouts and parsley, and season well.

6 When you are ready to serve the soup, stir in the basil leaves and ladle the soup into deep cups or bowls and garnish with sprigs of basil. Serve with a little grated Parmesan.

The pointed, spear-shaped leaves of sorrel are one of the first wild salad greens to appear in spring. They make a refreshingly sharp chilled soup.

SORREL SOUP

1 Finely shred the sorrel, then put it in a large pan with the onion and stock. Bring to the boil, then reduce the heat and simmer for 10–15 minutes.

2 Add the sugar and half the lemon juice to the pan, stir and simmer for a further 5–10 minutes.

3 In a bowl, beat the eggs and mix in the sour cream, then stir in about 250ml|8fl oz| 1 cup of the hot soup. Add another 250ml|8fl oz|1 cup of soup, stirring as you go to ensure a smooth texture.

4 Slowly pour the egg mixture into the hot soup, stirring constantly to prevent the eggs curdling and to ensure the texture remains smooth. Cook for just a few moments over a low heat until the soup thickens slightly. Season with a little salt to taste and stir in the remaining lemon juice.

5 Leave the soup to cool, then chill for at least 2 hours. Taste again for seasoning (it may need more salt or lemon juice) and serve sprinkled with the spring onions.

COOK'S TIP Shred the sorrel across the grain. This will help to prevent it from becoming stringy when it is cooked.

INGREDIENTS
serves four to six

500g | 1^1/$_4$lb sorrel leaves, stems removed

1 medium-large onion, thinly sliced

1.5 litres | 2^1/$_2$ pints | 6^1/$_4$ cups vegetable stock

15–30ml | 1–2 tbsp sugar

60ml | 4 tbsp lemon juice

2 eggs

150ml | ^{1}/$_4$ pint | ^{2}/$_3$ cup sour cream

salt

3–4 spring onions (scallions), thinly sliced, to garnish

Lightly cumin-spiced rice makes a fragrant filling for stuffed vine leaves, which is perfectly complemented by the new season's mint. It makes an ideal first course for a springtime lunch or dinner.

STUFFED VINE LEAVES with CUMIN and MINT

INGREDIENTS
serves six to eight

250g | 9oz | 1¹/₄ cups brown rice

30–45ml | 2–3 tbsp natural (plain) yogurt

3 garlic cloves, chopped

1 egg, lightly beaten

5–10ml | 1–2 tsp ground cumin

2.5ml | ¹/₂ tsp ground cinnamon

several handfuls of raisins

3–4 spring onions (scallions), thinly sliced

¹/₂ bunch fresh mint, plus extra to garnish

about 25 preserved or fresh vine leaves

salt, if necessary

8–10 unpeeled garlic cloves

juice of ¹/₂–1 lemon

90ml | 6 tbsp olive oil

for serving

1 lemon, cut into wedges or half slices

15–25 Greek black olives

150ml | ¹/₄ pint | ²/₃ cup natural yogurt

1 Put the rice in a pan with 300ml | ¹/₂ pint | 1¹/₄ cups water. Bring to the boil, reduce the heat, cover and simmer for 30 minutes, or until just tender. Drain well and leave to cool.

2 Put the cooked rice in a bowl, add the yogurt, garlic, egg, ground cumin and cinnamon, raisins, spring onions and mint and mix together.

3 If you are using preserved vine leaves, rinse them well. If using fresh vine leaves, blanch in salted boiling water for 2–3 minutes, then rinse under cold water and drain.

4 Lay the leaves on a board, shiny side down. Place 15–30ml | 1–2 tbsp of the mixture near the stalk of each leaf. Fold each one up, starting at the bottom, then the sides, and finally rolling up towards the top to enclose the filling.

5 Carefully layer the rolls in a steamer and stud with the whole garlic cloves. Fill the base of the steamer with water and drizzle the lemon juice and olive oil evenly over the rolls. Cover the steamer tightly and cook over a medium-high heat for about 40 minutes, adding more water to the steamer if necessary.

6 Remove the steamer from the heat and set aside to cool slightly. Arrange the vine leaves on a serving dish and serve hot or, alternatively, leave to cool completely. Garnish and serve with lemon wedges or half slices, olives and a bowl of yogurt, for dipping.

VARIATIONS For a twist to the classic stuffed vine leaf, other herbs such as dill or parsley can be used, and a handful of pine nuts can be added to the stuffing.

As the first lettuces appear, this traditional French way of braising them with peas and spring onions in butter makes a light side dish that is perfect with simply cooked fish or roast or grilled duck.

BRAISED LETTUCE and PEAS with MINT

INGREDIENTS
serves four

50g | 2oz | 1/4 cup butter

4 Little Gem (Bibb) lettuces, halved lengthways

2 bunches spring onions (scallions), trimmed and halved

5ml | 1 tsp caster (superfine) sugar

400g | 14oz | 3 1/2 cups fresh shelled or frozen peas

4 fresh mint sprigs

120ml | 4fl oz | 1/2 cup chicken or vegetable stock or water

salt and ground black pepper

15ml | 1 tbsp chopped fresh mint to garnish

1 Melt half the butter in a wide, heavy pan over a low heat. Add the prepared lettuces and spring onions.

2 Turn the vegetables in the butter, then sprinkle in the sugar, 2.5ml | 1/2 tsp salt and plenty of black pepper. Cover and cook very gently for 5 minutes, stirring once.

3 Add the peas and mint sprigs. Turn the peas in the buttery juices and pour in the stock or water, then cover and cook over a gentle heat for a further 5 minutes. Uncover and increase the heat to reduce the liquid to a few tablespoons.

4 Stir in the remaining butter and adjust the seasoning. Transfer to a warmed serving dish and sprinkle with the chopped mint. Serve immediately.

VARIATIONS
- Braise about 250g | 9oz baby carrots with the lettuce.
- Use 1 lettuce, shredding it coarsely, and omit the mint. Towards the end of cooking, stir in about 150g | 5oz rocket (arugula) – preferably the stronger-flavoured wild rocket – and cook briefly until wilted.
- Fry 115g | 4oz chopped smoked bacon or pancetta with 1 small chopped onion in the butter. Use 1 bunch of spring onions and omit the mint. Stir in some chopped parsley before serving. This version is also very good with small turnips, braised with lettuce.

Make the most of fresh globe artichokes as soon as they are available by serving them with this delicious garlic and mayonnaise dressing from Spain.

GLOBE ARTICHOKES with BEANS and AIOLI

1 First, make the aioli. Put the garlic and vinegar in a food processor or blender. With the motor running, slowly pour in the olive oil through the lid or feeder tube until the mixture is quite thick and smooth. (Alternatively, crush the garlic to a paste with the vinegar and gradually beat in the oil using a hand whisk.) Season with salt and pepper to taste.

2 Cook the green beans in lightly salted boiling water for 1–2 minutes, or until slightly softened. Drain well.

3 Trim the artichoke stalks close to the base. Cook the artichokes in a large pan of salted water for about 30 minutes, or until you can easily pull away a leaf from the base. Drain well.

4 Using a large, sharp knife, cut the artichokes in half lengthways and carefully scrape out the hairy choke using a teaspoon.

5 Arrange the artichokes and beans on serving plates and drizzle with the olive oil. Sprinkle the lemon rind over them and season to taste with coarse salt and a little pepper. Spoon the aioli into the artichoke hearts and serve the dish warm, garnished with lemon wedges.

6 To eat the artichokes, squeeze a little lemon juice over them, then pull the leaves from the base one at a time and use to scoop a little of the aioli sauce. Gently scrape away the fleshy end of each leaf with your teeth and discard the remainder of the leaf. Eat the tender base or "heart" of the artichoke with a knife and fork.

INGREDIENTS
serves three

225g | 8oz green beans

3 small globe artichokes

15ml | 1 tbsp olive oil

pared rind of 1 lemon

coarse salt, for sprinkling

lemon wedges, to garnish

for the aioli

6 large garlic cloves, thinly sliced

10ml | 2 tsp white wine vinegar

250ml | 8fl oz | 1 cup olive oil

salt and ground black pepper

As spring progresses towards summer, we look for lighter first courses and side dishes. The new season's asparagus is an ideal choice served with a tangy lemon and egg sauce.

ASPARAGUS with LEMON SAUCE

1 Cook the bundle of asparagus in salted boiling water for 7–10 minutes.

2 Drain well and arrange the asparagus in a serving dish. Reserve 200ml | 7fl oz | scant 1 cup of the cooking liquid.

3 Blend the cornflour with the cooled, reserved cooking liquid and place in a small pan. Bring to the boil, stirring constantly, and cook over a gentle heat until the sauce thickens slightly. Stir in the sugar, then remove the pan from the heat and allow to cool slightly.

4 Beat the egg yolks thoroughly with the lemon juice and stir gradually into the cooled sauce. Cook over a very low heat, stirring constantly, until the sauce is fairly thick. Be careful not to overheat the sauce or it may curdle. As soon as the sauce has thickened, remove the pan from the heat and continue stirring for 1 minute. Taste and add salt or sugar as necessary. Allow the sauce to cool slightly.

5 Stir the cooled sauce, then pour a little over the asparagus. Cover and chill for at least 2 hours before serving with the rest of the sauce.

VARIATIONS This sauce goes very well with all sorts of young vegetables. Try it with baby leeks, cooked whole or chopped, or serve it with other baby vegetables, such as carrots and courgettes (zucchini).

COOK'S TIP Use tiny asparagus spears for an elegant first course or a dinner party.

INGREDIENTS
serves four

675g | 1¹/₂lb asparagus, tough ends removed, and tied in a bundle

15ml | 1 tbsp cornflour (cornstarch)

about 10ml | 2 tsp sugar

2 egg yolks

juice of 1¹/₂ lemons

salt

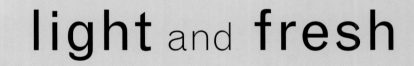

light and fresh

After comforting and substantial winter fare, we look
forward to cleaner flavours, buying what is plentiful
and cooking in new and imaginative ways. These light
meals and salads are designed for easy, one-course
eating that will fit in with your lifestyle.

Full of flavour, this easily prepared omelette makes a superb lunch or light supper and uses many of the season's ingredients.

SPRING VEGETABLE OMELETTE

INGREDIENTS
serves four

50g | 2oz | 1/2 cup fresh asparagus tips

50g | 2oz spring greens (collards), shredded

15ml | 1 tbsp sunflower oil

1 onion, sliced

175g | 6oz cooked new potatoes, halved or diced

2 tomatoes, chopped

6 eggs

15–30ml | 1–2 tbsp chopped fresh mixed herbs

salt and ground black pepper

salad, to serve

1 Steam the asparagus tips and spring greens over a pan of boiling water for 5–10 minutes, until tender. Drain the vegetables and keep them warm.

2 Heat the oil in a large frying pan that can safely be used under the grill (broiler). (Cover a wooden handle with foil to protect it.) Add the onion and cook over a low heat, stirring occasionally, for 5–10 minutes, until softened.

3 Add the new potatoes and cook, stirring constantly, for 3 minutes. Stir in the tomatoes, asparagus and spring greens. Beat the eggs lightly with the herbs and season to taste with salt and pepper.

4 Preheat the grill. Pour the egg mixture over the vegetables, then cook over a gentle heat until the base of the omelette is golden brown. Slide the pan under the grill and cook the omelette for 2–3 minutes, or until the top is golden brown. Serve immediately, cut into wedges, with salad.

White wine melds the flavours of bacon, spring greens and alliums in this light, spring dish. Serve with some crusty bread.

SPRING GREENS with BACON

1 In a large frying pan, heat the oil and butter and add the bacon. Fry for 2 minutes, then add the onions and fry for another 3 minutes, or until the onion begins to soften.

2 Add the wine and simmer vigorously for 2 minutes to reduce the liquid.

3 Reduce the heat and add the garlic, spring greens and salt and pepper. Cook over a low heat for about 15 minutes, or until the greens are tender. (Cover the pan so that the greens retain their colour.) Serve hot.

VARIATIONS If spring greens are difficult to get hold of, try other greens. Crisp curly kale or red or green cabbage will work well in this recipe. They may need a little longer cooking time and would stand up to a red wine.
• Likewise red or green chard, with its firm stems, or young spinach will do well but requires only the lightest cooking.
• Try this with mangetouts (snow peas) and white wine served with fresh, hot pasta.
• For a dinner party side dish, replace the bacon with chunks of pancetta.

INGREDIENTS
serves four

30ml | 2 tbsp olive oil

30ml | 2 tbsp butter

4 rashers (strips) bacon, chopped

1 large onion, thinly sliced

250ml | 8fl oz | 1 cup dry white wine

2 garlic cloves, finely chopped

900g | 2lb spring greens (collards), shredded

salt and ground black pepper

These melt-in-the-mouth herby spring onion fritters are excellent served with a fresh spicy salsa made with avocados, red onion and chilli.

RICOTTA and HERB FRITTERS

INGREDIENTS
serves four

250g | 9oz | generous 1 cup ricotta cheese

1 large (US extra large) egg, beaten

90ml | 6 tbsp self-raising (self-rising) flour

90ml | 6 tbsp milk

1 bunch spring onions (scallions), finely sliced

30ml | 2 tbsp chopped fresh coriander (cilantro)

sunflower oil, for shallow frying

salt and ground black pepper

200ml | 7fl oz | scant 1 cup crème fraîche, to serve

fresh coriander sprigs and lime wedges, to garnish

serve with fresh salsa

1 Beat the ricotta until smooth, then beat in the egg and flour, followed by the milk to make a smooth, thick batter. Beat in the spring onions and coriander. Season well with pepper and a little salt.

2 Heat a little oil in a non-stick frying pan over a medium heat. Add spoonfuls of the mixture to make fritters about 7.5cm | 3in across and fry for about 4–5 minutes each side, or until set and browned. The mixture makes 12 fritters.

3 Serve the fritters immediately, with salsa and a dollop of crème fraîche. Garnish with coriander sprigs and lime wedges.

COOK'S TIP Make a quick salsa by finely chopping avocado, red onion and fresh tomatoes. Add red chilli to taste and the juice and rind of a lime. Taste the salsa and adjust the seasoning, adding more lime juice and/or sugar to taste. You might like to add one or two teaspoons of Thai fish sauce if you have some. Leave for 30 minutes for the flavours to develop.

VARIATION The fritters are also good served with thinly sliced smoked salmon.

Grilling late-spring vegetables gives them a slight smokiness that goes very well with the sweetness of air-dried ham. Shaved Pecorino cheese adds a final flourish to the delicious flavours.

GRILLED GREENS with HAM and CHEESE

1 Cut off and discard the woody ends of the asparagus and use a vegetable peeler to peel the bottom 7.5cm|3in of the spears.

2 Preheat the grill (broiler). Toss the spring onions and asparagus in 30ml|2 tbsp of the oil. Place on two baking sheets and season with salt and pepper.

3 Grill (broil) the asparagus for 5 minutes on each side, or until just tender when tested with the tip of a sharp knife. Protect the tips with foil if they seem to char too much. Grill the spring onions for about 3–4 minutes on each side, or until tinged with brown. Brush both vegetables with more oil when you turn them.

4 Distribute the vegetables among four to six plates. Season with pepper, and drizzle over the vinegar. Lay two to three slices of ham on each plate and shave the Pecorino over the top. Serve more extra virgin olive oil for drizzling at the table.

COOK'S TIPS The spring onions can be cooked on a cast-iron ridged griddle. If more convenient, the asparagus can be roasted at 200°C|400°F|Gas 6 for 15 minutes.

INGREDIENTS
serves four to six

500g|1¼lb asparagus

2 bunches plump spring onions (scallions) (about 24)

45–60ml|3–4 tbsp extra virgin olive oil

20ml|4 tsp balsamic vinegar

8–12 slices prosciutto or San Daniele ham

50g|2oz Pecorino cheese

salt and ground black pepper

extra virgin olive oil, to serve

A richly flavoured tomato sauce with garlic, fennel and artichokes makes a fine accompaniment for penne. This is the perfect dish to serve when globe artichokes are in season.

ARTICHOKES with PENNE

INGREDIENTS
serves six

juice of 1 lemon

2 globe artichokes

30ml | 2 tbsp olive oil

1 small fennel bulb, thinly sliced, with feathery tops reserved

1 onion, finely chopped

4 garlic cloves, finely chopped

1 handful fresh flat leaf parsley, coarsely chopped

400g | 14oz can chopped plum tomatoes

150ml | ¼ pint | ⅔ cup dry white wine

350g | 12oz | 3 cups dried penne

10ml | 2 tsp capers, chopped

salt and ground black pepper

freshly grated Parmesan cheese, to serve

1 Fill a large mixing bowl with cold water and add half the lemon juice. To prepare the artichokes, cut or break off the stalks, then pull off and discard the outer leaves until only the pale inner leaves remain. Cut off the tops of these leaves, cut the base in half lengthways, then prise the hairy choke out of the centre with the tip of the knife and discard. Cut the artichoke lengthways into 5mm | ¼in pieces, adding them immediately to the bowl of acidulated water to prevent them discolouring.

2 Bring a large pan of salted water to the boil. Drain the artichokes and add them immediately to the water. Boil for 5 minutes, then drain and set aside. Heat the oil in a large pan and add the fennel, onion, garlic and parsley. Cook over a low to medium heat, stirring frequently, for 10 minutes, or until the fennel has softened and is lightly coloured.

3 Add the tomatoes and wine, with seasoning to taste. Bring to the boil, stirring, then lower the heat, cover and simmer for 10–15 minutes. Stir in the artichokes, replace the lid and simmer for 10 minutes more. Meanwhile, add the pasta to a large pan of lightly salted boiling water and cook according to the instructions on the packet.

4 Drain the pasta, reserving a little of the cooking water. Add the capers to the sauce, stir well then taste for seasoning. Add the remaining lemon juice. Tip the pasta into a warmed serving bowl, pour the sauce over and toss thoroughly to mix, adding a little of the reserved cooking water if you like a thinner sauce. Serve immediately, garnished with the reserved fennel fronds. Hand around a bowl of grated Parmesan separately.

Baby spinach leaves and creamy avocado are given a sharp tang by the simple lemon dressing in this refreshing spring salad with crunchy polenta croûtons.

SPINACH and AVOCADO SALAD

1 Preheat the oven to 200°C | 400°F | Gas 6. Place the onion wedges and polenta cubes on a lightly oiled baking sheet and bake for 25 minutes, or until the onion is tender and the polenta is crisp and golden, turning them regularly to prevent them sticking. Leave to cool slightly.

2 Meanwhile, make the dressing. Place the olive oil, lemon juice and seasoning to taste in a bowl or screw-top jar. Stir or shake thoroughly to combine.

3 Place the spinach leaves in a serving bowl. Toss the avocado in the lemon juice to prevent it browning, then add to the spinach with the roasted onions.

4 Pour the dressing over the salad and toss gently to combine. Sprinkle the polenta croûtons on top or hand them round separately, and serve immediately.

COOK'S TIP If you can't find ready-made polenta, you can make your own using instant polenta grains. Simply cook according to the packet instructions, then pour into a tray and leave to cool and set.

INGREDIENTS
serves four

1 large red onion, cut into wedges

350g | 12oz ready-made polenta, cut into 1cm | 1/2in cubes

olive oil, for brushing

225g | 8oz baby spinach leaves

1 avocado, peeled, stoned (pitted) and sliced

5ml | 1 tsp lemon juice

for the dressing

60ml | 4 tbsp extra virgin olive oil

juice of 1/2 lemon

salt and ground black pepper

As late spring days become warmer, it may feel too warm for big pasta dishes. Try serving tagliatelle as a warm salad combined with ham, eggs and asparagus.

WARM TAGLIATELLE SALAD with ASPARAGUS

INGREDIENTS
serves four

450g | 1lb asparagus

450g | 1lb dried tagliatelle

225g | 8oz cooked ham, in 5mm | 1/4in thick slices, cut into fingers

2 eggs, hard-boiled and sliced

50g | 2oz Parmesan cheese, shaved

salt and ground black pepper

for the dressing

50g | 2oz cooked potato

75ml | 5 tbsp olive oil

15ml | 1 tbsp lemon juice

10ml | 2 tsp Dijon mustard

120ml | 4fl oz | 1/2 cup vegetable stock

1 Trim and discard the tough woody part of the asparagus. Cut the spears in half and cook the thicker halves in salted boiling water for 12 minutes. After 6 minutes add the tips. Drain, then refresh under cold water until warm.

2 Finely chop 150g | 5oz of the thick asparagus pieces. Place in a food processor with the dressing ingredients and process until smooth.

3 Boil the pasta in a large pan of salted water according to the packet instructions until tender. Refresh under cold water until warm, and drain.

4 To serve, toss the pasta with the asparagus sauce and divide among four pasta plates. Top with the ham, hard-boiled eggs and asparagus tips. Serve with a sprinkling of Parmesan cheese shavings.

VARIATIONS Use sliced chicken instead of the ham, or thin slices of softer Italian cheese, such as Fontina or Asiago.

tender and tasty

From spring lamb and chicken to Dover sole and scallops, there is a wide selection of good-quality meat, fish and poultry available at this time of year. Instead of hunting for a particular ingredient, take advantage of what is plentiful and substitute what looks good and fresh in the shops.

For a light springtime meal, try crisply coated plaice or flounder served with a simple tomato sauce. It makes a delicious choice for a family supper.

FRIED FISH with TOMATO SAUCE

INGREDIENTS
serves four

25g | 1oz | ¼ cup plain (all-purpose) flour

2 eggs, beaten

75g | 3oz | generous 1 cup dried breadcrumbs, preferably home-made

4 small plaice or flounder, skin removed

15g | ½oz | 1 tbsp butter

15ml | 1 tbsp sunflower oil

salt and ground black pepper

1 lemon, quartered, to serve

fresh basil leaves, to garnish

for the sauce

30ml | 2 tbsp olive oil

1 red onion, finely chopped

1 garlic clove, finely chopped

400g | 14oz can chopped tomatoes

15ml | 1 tbsp tomato purée (paste)

15ml | 1 tbsp torn fresh basil leaves

1 First make the tomato sauce. Heat the olive oil in a large pan, add the finely chopped onion and garlic and cook gently for about 5 minutes, or until softened and pale golden. Stir in the chopped tomatoes and tomato purée and simmer for 20–30 minutes, stirring occasionally. Season with salt and pepper and stir in the basil.

2 Spread out the flour in a shallow dish, pour the beaten eggs into another and spread out the breadcrumbs in a third. Season the plaice or flounder with salt and pepper.

3 Hold a fish in your left hand and dip first in flour, then in egg and finally in the breadcrumbs, patting the crumbs on with your dry right hand.

4 Heat the butter and oil in a frying pan until foaming. Fry the fish one at a time in the hot fat for about 5 minutes on each side, or until golden brown and cooked through but still juicy in the middle. Drain on kitchen paper and keep hot while you fry the rest. Serve with lemon wedges and the tomato sauce, garnished with basil leaves.

VARIATIONS This recipe works equally well with lemon sole or dabs (these do not need skinning), or fillets of haddock and whiting.

Thai flavourings add a new dimension to the delicate taste and texture of Dover sole. Lightly steamed in lettuce and accompanied by mussels, it makes a tasty and unusual dish.

STEAMED LETTUCE-WRAPPED SOLE

INGREDIENTS
serves four

2 large Dover or lemon sole fillets, skinned

15ml | 1 tbsp sesame seeds

15ml | 1 tbsp sunflower or groundnut (peanut) oil

10ml | 2 tsp sesame oil

2.5cm | 1in piece fresh root ginger, peeled and grated

3 garlic cloves, finely chopped

15ml | 1 tbsp soy sauce or Thai fish sauce

juice of 1 lemon

2 spring onions (scallions), thinly sliced

8 large soft lettuce leaves

12 large fresh mussels, scrubbed and bearded

1 Cut the sole fillets in half lengthways. Season and set aside. Prepare a steamer.

2 Heat a heavy frying pan until hot. Toast the sesame seeds lightly and set aside.

3 Heat the oils in the frying pan over a medium heat. Add the ginger and garlic and cook until lightly coloured. Stir in the soy sauce or Thai fish sauce, lemon juice and spring onions. Remove from the heat, and stir in the sesame seeds.

4 Lay the pieces of fish on baking parchment, skinned side up. Spread each evenly with the ginger mixture. Roll up each piece, starting at the tail end. Place on a baking sheet.

5 Plunge the lettuce leaves into the boiling water you have prepared for the steamer and immediately lift them out with tongs or a slotted spoon. Lay them out flat on kitchen paper and gently pat them dry. Wrap each sole parcel in two lettuce leaves, making sure that the filling is well covered to keep it in place.

6 Arrange the fish parcels in a steamer basket. Cover and steam over simmering water for 8 minutes. Discard any opened mussels that do not close when sharply tapped. Add the mussels, and steam for 2–4 minutes, or until opened. Discard any that remain closed. Put the parcels on individual warmed plates, halve and garnish with mussels. Serve immediately.

VARIATION Trout, plaice, flounder or brill are all excellent cooked this way.

This Jewish dish of fresh tuna and peas is enjoyed in Italy at Pesach (Passover), which falls in spring, served with matzo pancakes. Garlic, parsley and a hint of fennel give the tuna an unusual and appetizing flavour.

TONNO CON PISELLI

1 Preheat the oven to 190°C | 375°F | Gas 5. Heat the olive oil in a large frying pan, then add the chopped onion, garlic, flat leaf parsley and fennel seeds, and fry over a low heat for about 5 minutes, or until the onion is softened but not browned.

2 Sprinkle the tuna steaks on each side with salt and pepper. Add to the pan and cook for 2–3 minutes on each side, or until lightly browned. Transfer the tuna steaks to a shallow baking dish, in a single layer.

3 Add the canned tomatoes along with their juice and the wine or fish stock to the onions and cook over a medium heat for 5–10 minutes, stirring, until the flavours blend together and the mixture thickens slightly.

4 Stir the tomato purée, sugar, if needed, and salt and pepper into the tomato sauce, then add the fresh or frozen peas. Pour the mixture over the fish steaks and bake, uncovered, for about 10 minutes, or until tender. Serve with traditional matzo pancakes or use pitta or another flatbread.

VARIATIONS Use tuna fillets in place of the steaks or try different fish steaks, such as salmon or swordfish.

INGREDIENTS
serves four

60ml | 4 tbsp olive oil

1 onion, chopped

4–5 garlic cloves, chopped

45ml | 3 tbsp chopped fresh flat leaf parsley

1–2 pinches of fennel seeds

350g | 12oz tuna steaks

400g | 14oz can chopped tomatoes

120ml | 4fl oz | 1/2 cup dry white wine or fish stock

30–45ml | 2–3 tbsp tomato purée (paste)

pinch of sugar, if needed

350g | 12oz | 3 cups fresh shelled peas

salt and ground black pepper

Scallops are one of the most delicious shellfish and are available throughout the spring. Here they are partnered with a delicious chive sauce and a pilaff of wild and white rice with sweet leeks and carrots.

SCALLOPS with LEEK and CARROT RICE

1 Lightly season the scallops, brush with 15ml | 1 tbsp of the olive oil and set aside. Cook the wild rice in plenty of boiling water for about 30 minutes, or until tender, then drain.

2 Melt half the butter in a small frying pan and cook the carrots gently for 4–5 minutes. Add the leeks and fry for another 2 minutes. Season and add 30–45ml | 2–3 tbsp water, then cover and cook for a few minutes more. Uncover and cook until the liquid has reduced. Remove from the heat.

3 Melt half the remaining butter with 15ml | 1 tbsp of the remaining oil in a heavy pan. Add the onion and fry for 3–4 minutes, or until softened but not browned. Add the long grain rice and bay leaf and cook, stirring constantly, until the rice looks translucent and the grains are coated with oil.

4 Pour in half the wine and stock. Add 2.5ml | 1/2 tsp salt and bring to the boil. Stir, then cover and cook gently for 15 minutes, or until the liquid is absorbed and the rice is tender. Reheat the carrots and leeks, then stir them into the long grain rice with the wild rice. Adjust the seasoning.

5 Pour the remaining wine and stock into a small pan and boil rapidly until reduced by half. Heat a heavy frying pan over a high heat. Add the remaining butter and oil. Sear the scallops for 1–2 minutes each side, then set aside and keep warm.

6 Pour the reduced stock into the pan and heat until bubbling, then add the cream and boil until thickened. Season and add lemon juice, chives and scallops. Stir the chervil into the rice. Serve the rice with the scallops on top and spoon the sauce over.

INGREDIENTS
serves four

12–16 shelled scallops

45ml | 3 tbsp olive oil

50g | 2oz | 1/3 cup wild rice

65g | 2 1/2oz | 5 tbsp butter

4 carrots, cut into long thin strips

2 leeks, cut into thick, diagonal slices

1 small onion, finely chopped

115g | 4oz | 2/3 cup long grain rice

1 fresh bay leaf

200ml | 7fl oz | scant 1 cup white wine

450ml | 3/4 pint | scant 2 cups fish stock

60ml | 4 tbsp double (heavy) cream

a little lemon juice

25ml | 1 1/2 tbsp chopped fresh chives

30ml | 2 tbsp chervil sprigs

salt and ground black pepper

A lovely wine and herb-scented stock contains tender morsels of chicken and baby vegetables in this light and aromatic seasonal version of the French casserole.

CHICKEN POT AU FEU

INGREDIENTS
serves four

1 chicken, about 2.25kg | 5lb

1 parsley sprig

15ml | 1 tbsp black peppercorns

1 bay leaf

300g | 11oz baby carrots, washed and left whole

175g | 6oz baby leeks, washed and left whole

25g | 1oz | 2 tbsp butter

15ml | 1 tbsp olive oil

300g | 11oz shallots, halved if large

200ml | 7fl oz | scant 1 cup dry white wine

800g | 1³/₄lb baby new potatoes

120ml | 4fl oz | ¹/₂ cup double (heavy) cream

salt and ground black pepper

small bunch parsley or tarragon, chopped, to garnish

1 Joint the chicken into eight pieces and place the carcass in a large stockpot. Add the parsley sprig, peppercorns, bay leaf and the trimmings from the carrots and leeks. Cover with cold water and bring to the boil. Simmer for 45 minutes, then strain.

2 Meanwhile, melt the butter with the olive oil in a frying pan, then add the chicken pieces. Add seasoning, and brown the chicken all over. Transfer the chicken pieces to a plate and add the shallots to the pan. Cook over a low heat for 20 minutes, stirring occasionally, until softened, but not browned.

3 Return the chicken to the pan and add the wine. Scrape up any juices from the bottom of the pan with a wooden spoon, then add the carrots, leeks and potatoes with enough of the stock to just cover. Bring to the boil, then cover and simmer for 20 minutes. Stir in the cream.

4 Transfer to a serving dish and garnish with the herbs. Serve immediately.

Tender poussins are spatchcocked and grilled with a garlic and spring herb butter, making this a light and extremely tasty dish that is quick to cook.

SPATCHCOCK POUSSINS with SPRING HERBS

INGREDIENTS
serves two

2 poussins, each weighing about 450g | 1lb

1 shallot, finely chopped

2 garlic cloves, crushed

45ml | 3 tbsp chopped mixed fresh herbs, such as flat leaf parsley, sage, rosemary and thyme

75g | 3oz | 6 tbsp butter, softened

salt and ground black pepper

1 To spatchcock a poussin, place it breast down on a chopping board and split it along the back. Open out the bird and turn it over, so that the breast side is uppermost. Press the bird as flat as possible, then thread two metal skewers through it, across the breast and thigh, to keep it flat. Repeat with the second poussin and place the skewered birds on a large grill (broiling) pan.

2 Add the chopped shallot, crushed garlic and chopped mixed herbs to the butter with plenty of seasoning, and then beat well. Dot the butter over the spatchcock poussins.

3 Preheat the grill (broiler) to high and cook the poussins for 30 minutes, turning them over halfway through. Turn again and baste with the cooking juices, then cook for a further 5–7 minutes on each side.

VARIATIONS The addition of some finely chopped chilli or a little grated lemon rind to the butter will give it a lift.

Mild, sweet leeks and tender baby vegetables are excellent braised in wine with prime guinea fowl flavoured with mustard and mint.

GUINEA FOWL with BABY VEGETABLES

1 Heat 30ml|2 tbsp of the oil in a large frying pan and cook the pancetta over a medium heat until lightly browned, stirring occasionally. Remove the pancetta and set aside.

2 Season the flour with salt and pepper and toss the guinea fowl portions in it. Fry in the oil remaining in the pan until browned on all sides. Transfer to a flameproof casserole. Preheat the oven to 180°C|350°F|Gas 4.

3 Add the remaining oil to the pan and cook the onion gently until soft. Add the garlic and fry for 3–4 minutes, then stir in the pancetta and wine. Tie the thyme, bay leaf and parsley into a bundle and add to the pan. Bring to the boil, then simmer gently for 3–4 minutes. Pour over the guinea fowl in the casserole dish and add seasoning. Cover and cook in the oven for 40 minutes.

4 Add the baby carrots and turnips to the casserole and cook, covered, for another 30 minutes, or until the vegetables are just tender. Stir in the leeks and cook for a further 15–20 minutes, or until all the vegetables are fully cooked.

5 Meanwhile, blanch the peas in boiling water for 2 minutes, then drain. Transfer the guinea fowl and vegetables to a warmed serving dish. Place the casserole on the hob and boil the juices vigorously over a high heat until they are reduced by about half.

6 Stir in the peas and cook gently for 2–3 minutes, then stir in the mustard and adjust the seasoning. Stir in most of the parsley and the mint. Pour this sauce over the guinea fowl, scatter the remaining parsley over the top and serve immediately.

INGREDIENTS
serves four

45ml|3 tbsp olive oil

115g|4oz pancetta, cut into lardons

30ml|2 tbsp plain (all-purpose) flour

2 1.2–1.6kg|2¹/₂–3¹/₂lb guinea fowl, each jointed into 4 portions

1 onion, chopped

1 head of garlic, separated into cloves and peeled

1 bottle dry white wine

fresh thyme sprig

1 fresh bay leaf

a few parsley stalks

250g|9oz baby carrots

250g|9oz baby turnips

6 slender leeks, cut into 7.5cm|3in lengths

250g|9oz|2¹/₄ cups fresh shelled peas

15ml|1 tbsp French herb mustard

15g|¹/₂oz|¹/₄ cup chopped flat leaf parsley

15ml|1 tbsp chopped fresh mint

salt and ground black pepper

Prepare this classic Greek dish when young lamb is at its best and lettuces and fresh dill are available. The unusual flavours make it an ideal choice for a dinner party, and it can also be cooked in advance.

COS LETTUCE and LAMB CASSEROLE

1 Heat the olive oil in a large, heavy pan. Add the chopped onion and sauté for 3–5 minutes, or until it glistens and becomes translucent.

2 Increase the heat, then add the lamb steaks and cook, turning them over frequently, until all the moisture has been driven off, a process that will take about 15 minutes.

3 Add salt to taste and enough hot water to cover the meat. Cover the pan and simmer for about 1 hour, until the meat is only just tender.

4 Add the lettuces, spring onions and dill. If necessary, pour in a little more hot water so that all the vegetables are almost covered. Replace the lid on the pan and simmer for 15–20 minutes more. Remove from the heat and let the dish stand for 5 minutes while you prepare the ingredients for the sauce.

5 Beat the eggs lightly in a bowl, add the cornflour mixture and beat until smooth. Add the lemon juice and whisk briefly, then continue to whisk while gradually adding 75–90ml/5–6 tbsp of the hot liquid from the pan containing the lamb.

6 Pour the sauce over the meat. Do not stir; instead gently shake and rotate the pan until the sauce is incorporated with the remaining liquid. Return the pan to a gentle heat for 2–3 minutes, just long enough to warm the sauce through. Do not let it boil, or the sauce is likely to curdle. Serve on warmed plates and scatter over some extra chopped dill.

INGREDIENTS
serves four to six

45ml | 3 tbsp olive oil

1 onion, chopped

1kg | 2¼lb boned leg of lamb, sliced into 4–6 medium steaks

2 cos or romaine lettuces, coarsely shredded

6 spring onions (scallions), sliced

60ml | 4 tbsp roughly chopped fresh dill, plus extra to garnish (optional)

for the sauce

2 eggs

15ml | 1 tbsp cornflour (cornstarch), mixed to a paste with 120ml | 4fl oz | ½ cup water

juice of 1 lemon

salt

Fresh herbs and garlic add depth of flavour to this rack of lamb, which is served with Puy lentils in a rich tomato sauce. Serve with potatoes and steamed spring vegetables.

HERB-CRUSTED RACK of LAMB

INGREDIENTS
serves four

2 six-bone racks of lamb, chined

50g | 2oz | 1 cup fresh white breadcrumbs

2 large garlic cloves, crushed

90ml | 6 tbsp chopped mixed fresh herbs, such as rosemary, thyme, flat leaf parsley and marjoram, plus extra sprigs to garnish

50g | 2oz | 1/4 cup butter, melted

salt and ground black pepper

new potatoes, to serve

for the Puy lentils

1 red onion, chopped

30ml | 2 tbsp olive oil

400g | 14oz can Puy or green lentils, rinsed and drained

400g | 14oz can chopped tomatoes

30ml | 2 tbsp chopped fresh parsley

1 Preheat the oven to 220°C | 425°F | Gas 7. Trim any excess fat from the lamb, season well with salt and pepper.

2 Mix together the breadcrumbs, garlic, herbs and butter, and press on to the fat side of the lamb. Place in a roasting pan and roast for 25 minutes. Cover with foil, and allow to stand for 5 minutes before carving.

3 To make the Puy lentils, cook the onion in the olive oil until softened. Add the lentils and tomatoes and cook gently for 5 minutes, or until the lentils are piping hot. Stir in the parsley and season to taste.

4 Cut each rack of lamb in half and serve with the lentils and new potatoes. Garnish with herb sprigs.

sweet and tart

Here are cakes and desserts that make the most of the clean, sharp-tasting seasonal goodies. Some treats like rhubarb have a very short season so enjoy those tender pink shoots while you can. More fruit than you can eat? Then preserve it by making ice cream to enjoy later in the year.

Tender, slow-cooked orange gives this moist cake its fragrance. Serve with coffee, afternoon tea or with whipped cream for a perfect springtime dessert.

MOIST ORANGE and ALMOND CAKE

INGREDIENTS
serves eight

1 large Valencia or Navelina orange

butter, for greasing

3 eggs

225g | 8oz | generous 1 cup caster (superfine) sugar

5ml | 1 tsp baking powder

225g | 8oz | 2 cups ground almonds

25g | 1oz | 1/4 cup plain (all-purpose) flour

icing (confectioners') sugar, for dusting

1 Pierce the orange with a skewer. Put it in a deep pan and pour over water to cover it. Bring to the boil, then cover and simmer for 1 hour until the skin is soft. Drain, then cool.

2 Preheat the oven to 180°C | 350°F | Gas 4. Lightly grease a 20cm | 8in round cake tin (pan) and line it with baking parchment. Cut the cooled orange in half and discard all the pips (seeds). Place the orange, peel, skin and all, in a food processor or blender and purée until smooth and pulpy.

3 In a bowl, whisk the eggs and caster sugar until thick. Fold in the baking powder, almonds and flour. Fold in the purée.

4 Pour into the prepared tin, level the surface and bake for 1 hour, or until a skewer inserted into the middle comes out clean. Cool the cake in the tin for 10 minutes, then turn out on to a wire rack, peel off the lining paper and cool completely. Dust the top liberally with icing sugar and serve.

COOK'S TIP To make a delicious dessert, tuck orange slices underneath the cake just before serving with whipped cream.

The sharp tang of spring rhubarb with this sweet meringue topping will really tantalize the taste buds. Delicious hot or cold with cream or vanilla ice cream.

RHUBARB MERINGUE PIE

1 Sift the flour into a bowl and add the ground walnuts. Rub in the butter until the mixture resembles very fine breadcrumbs. Stir in 30ml|2 tbsp of the sugar with 1 egg yolk beaten with 15ml|1 tbsp water. Mix to a firm dough. Turn out on to a floured surface and knead lightly. Wrap in a plastic bag and chill for at least 30 minutes.

2 Preheat the oven to 190°C|375°F|Gas 5. Roll out the pastry on a lightly floured surface and use to line a 23cm|9in fluted flan tin (tart pan). Prick the base with a fork. Line the pastry with baking parchment and fill with baking beans. Bake for 15 minutes.

3 Meanwhile, put the rhubarb, 75g|3oz|6 tbsp of the remaining sugar and the orange rind in a pan. Cover with a lid and cook over a low heat until the rhubarb is tender.

4 Remove the beans and paper from the pastry case, then brush all over with a little of the remaining egg yolk. Bake for 10–15 minutes, or until the pastry is crisp.

5 Blend together the cornflour and the orange juice in a small bowl. Remove from the heat, stir the cornflour mixture into the cooked rhubarb, then bring to the boil, stirring constantly until thickened. Cook for a further 1–2 minutes. Cool slightly, then beat in the remaining egg yolks. Pour into the flan case.

6 Whisk the egg whites until they form soft peaks, then whisk in the remaining sugar, 15ml|1 tbsp at time, whisking well after each addition.

7 Swirl the meringue over the filling to cover completely. Bake for 25 minutes, or until golden. Serve warm, or leave to cool, and serve with whipped cream.

INGREDIENTS
serves six

200g|7oz|1³/4 cups plain (all-purpose) flour, plus extra for dusting

25g|1oz|¹/4 cup ground walnuts

115g|4oz|¹/2 cup butter, diced

275g|10oz|1¹/2 cups caster (superfine) sugar

4 egg yolks

675g|1¹/2lb rhubarb, cut into small pieces

finely grated rind and juice of 3 blood or navel oranges

75ml|5 tbsp cornflour (cornstarch)

3 egg whites

whipped cream, to serve

Use fresh free-range eggs with golden yolks for this tart if you can, as their colour will add to the look of the finished dessert. It is very lemony, so serve with cream or vanilla ice.

CLASSIC LEMON TART

INGREDIENTS
serves eight

150g | 5oz | 1¼ cups plain (all-purpose) flour, sifted

50g | 2oz | ½ cup hazelnuts, toasted and finely ground

175g | 6oz | scant 1 cup caster (superfine) sugar

115g | 4oz | ½ cup unsalted (sweet) butter, softened

4 eggs

finely grated rind of 2 lemons and at least 175ml | 6fl oz | ¾ cup lemon juice

150ml | ¼ pint | ⅔ cup double (heavy) cream

1 Mix together the flour, nuts and 25g | 1oz | 2 tbsp sugar, then gently work in the butter and, if necessary, 15–30ml | 1–2 tbsp cold water to make a soft dough. Chill for 10 minutes. Roll out the dough and use to line a 20cm | 8in loose-based flan tin (tart pan). If you find it too difficult to roll out, push the pastry into the flan tin. Chill for about 20 minutes. Preheat the oven to 200°C | 400°F | Gas 6.

2 Line the pastry case with baking parchment, fill with baking beans, and bake for 15 minutes. Remove the paper and beans, and cook for a further 5–10 minutes, or until the base is crisp.

3 Beat the eggs, lemon rind and juice, the remaining sugar and cream until well blended. Pour into the pastry case. Bake for about 30 minutes, or until just set.

COOK'S TIP When working with fragile pastry like this, try rolling it out over the loose base of the flan tin, ready to lift it up and carefully ease it into the tin surround.

Full-flavoured Alphonso mangoes, which are available in late spring, are best for this dish if you can locate them.

GRIDDLED MANGO with LIME SYRUP SORBET

1 Place the sugar in a heavy pan and add 250ml | 8fl oz | 1 cup water. Heat gently until the sugar has dissolved. Increase the heat and boil for 5 minutes. Cool completely. Add the lime juice and any pulp that has collected in the squeezer. Strain the mixture and reserve 200ml | 7fl oz | scant 1 cup in a bowl with the star anise.

2 Pour the remaining liquid into a measuring jug or cup and make up to 600ml | 1 pint | 2½ cups with cold water. Mix well.

3 BY HAND: pour into a freezerproof container. Freeze for 1½ hours, stir well and return to the freezer for another hour until set. Transfer the sorbet mixture to a food processor and pulse to a smooth ice purée. Freeze for another hour or longer, if wished.
USING AN ICE CREAM MAKER: pour the liquid into the bowl and churn until thick. Transfer to a freezerproof container and freeze for at least 30 minutes before serving.

4 Pour the reserved syrup into a pan and boil for 2–3 minutes, or until thickened a little. Leave to cool. Cut the cheeks from either side of the stone (pit) on each unpeeled mango, and score the flesh on each in a diamond pattern. Brush with a little oil. Heat a griddle, until very hot and a few drops of water sprinkled on the surface evaporate instantly. Lower the heat a little and griddle the mango halves, cut side down, for 30–60 seconds until branded with golden griddle marks.

5 Invert the mango cheeks on individual plates and serve hot or cold with the syrup drizzled over and a scoop or two of sorbet. Decorate with the reserved star anise.

INGREDIENTS
serves six

250g | 9oz | 1¼ cups sugar

juice of 6 limes

3 star anise

6 small or 3 medium to large mangoes

groundnut (peanut) oil, for brushing

Exotic fruits are the perfect choice for a refreshing fruit salad, especially when they are flavoured and sweetened with lime and coffee liqueur.

FRAGRANT FRUIT SALAD

INGREDIENTS
serves six

130g | 4¹/₂oz | scant ³/₄ cup sugar

thinly pared rind and juice of 1 lime

60ml | 4 tbsp coffee liqueur, such as Tia Maria, Kahlúa or Toussaint

1 small pineapple

1 papaya

2 pomegranates

1 medium mango

2 passion fruits

fine strips of lime peel, to decorate

1 Put the sugar and lime rind in a small pan with 150ml | ¹/₄ pint | ²/₃ cup water. Heat gently until the sugar dissolves, then bring to the boil and simmer for 5 minutes. Leave to cool, then strain into a large serving bowl. Stir in the lime juice and liqueur.

2 Using a sharp knife, cut the plume and stalk end from the pineapple. Peel thickly and cut the flesh into bitesize pieces, discarding the woody central core. Add to the bowl.

3 Cut the papaya in half and scoop out the seeds. Cut away the skin, then cut into slices. Cut the pomegranates in half and scoop out the seeds. Break into clusters and add to the bowl.

4 Cut the mango lengthways, along each side of the stone (pit). Peel the skin off the flesh. Cut into slices and add with the rest of the fruit to the bowl. Stir well.

5 Halve the passion fruits and scoop out the flesh using a teaspoon. Spoon over the salad and serve, decorated with fine strips of lime peel.

COOK'S TIP To maximize the flavour of the fruit, allow the salad to stand at room temperature for an hour before serving.

Make the most of rhubarb's short season by enjoying this classic combination of rhubarb and ginger in a mouthwatering ice cream made with mascarpone.

RHUBARB and GINGER ICE CREAM

INGREDIENTS
serves four to six

5 pieces of preserved stem ginger

450g | 1lb trimmed rhubarb, sliced

115g | 4oz | generous 1/2 cup caster (superfine) sugar

30ml | 2 tbsp water

150g | 5oz | 2/3 cup mascarpone

150ml | 1/4 pint | 2/3 cup whipping cream

wafer baskets, to serve (optional)

1 Using a sharp knife, roughly chop the stem ginger and set it aside. Put the rhubarb slices into a pan and add the sugar and water. Cover and simmer for 5 minutes, or until the rhubarb is just tender and still bright pink.

2 Tip the mixture into a food processor or blender. Process until smooth, leave to cool and then chill.

3 BY HAND: mix together the mascarpone, cream and ginger with the rhubarb purée.
USING AN ICE CREAM MAKER: churn the rhubarb purée for 15–20 minutes, or until it is thick.

4 BY HAND: pour the mixture into a plastic tub or similar freezerproof container and freeze for 6 hours, or until firm, beating once or twice during the freezing time to break up the ice crystals.
USING AN ICE CREAM MAKER: put the mascarpone into a bowl, soften it with a wooden spoon, then gradually beat in the cream. Add the chopped ginger, then transfer to the ice cream maker and churn until the ice cream is firm.

5 Serve as scoops in bowls or wafer baskets or cups.

COOK'S TIP If the rhubarb purée is rather pale, add a few drops of pink colouring when mixing in the cream.

This refreshing sorbet is perfect for a lazy afternoon in the garden.

MINTED EARL GREY SORBET

1 Put the caster sugar and water into a pan and bring the mixture to the boil, stirring until the sugar has dissolved.

2 Thinly pare the rind from the lemon so that it falls straight into the pan of syrup. Simmer for 2 minutes then pour into a bowl. Cool, and then chill.

3 Put the tea into a pan and pour on the boiling water. Cover and leave to stand for 5 minutes, then strain into a bowl. Cool, and then chill.

4 BY HAND: pour the tea into a plastic tub or similar freezerproof container. Strain in the chilled syrup. Freeze for 4 hours.
USING AN ICE CREAM MAKER: combine the tea and syrup and churn the mixture until thick.

5 BY HAND: lightly whisk the egg white until just frothy. Scoop the sorbet into a food processor, process until smooth and mix in the mint and egg white. Spoon back into the tub and freeze for 4 hours, or until firm.
USING AN ICE CREAM MAKER: add the mint to the mixture. Lightly whisk the egg white until just frothy, then tip it into the ice cream maker and continue to churn until firm enough to scoop.

6 Serve in scoops, decorated with a few fresh or frosted mint leaves.

COOK'S TIP If you have only Earl Grey tea bags these can be used instead, but add enough to make 450ml|³/₄ pint|scant 2 cups strong tea. Make frosted mint leaves to serve by dipping the leaves in egg white and sprinkling them with caster sugar.

INGREDIENTS
serves six

200g | 7oz | 1 cup caster (superfine) sugar

300ml | ¹/₂ pint | 1¹/₄ cups water

1 lemon, well scrubbed

45ml | 3 tbsp Earl Grey tea leaves

450ml | ³/₄ pint | scant 2 cups boiling water

1 egg white

30ml | 2 tbsp chopped fresh mint leaves

fresh mint sprigs or frosted mint, to decorate

INDEX